Sutton-in-Ashfield

with
Huthwaite and Star

on old picture pos

David Ottewe..

1. St. Mary's Church: the octagonal spire was erected in 1818 to replace an earlier structure which was storm-damaged. The tower has eight bells, three of which are a memorial to the Great War dead, two for the Second World War fallen. This card was published by Valentine & Sons Ltd.

Designed and Published by
Reflections of a Bygone Age
Keyworth, Nottingham 1993

Reprinted 2000

ISBN 0 946245 80 0

Printed by
Adlard Print and Typesetting Services,
Ruddington, Notts.

2. Postcard by C. & A.G. Lewis from the early 1920s shows a deserted Church Street.

COPYRIGHT
SIA- 21   S. MICHAEL'S   THE CHURCH. SUTTON-IN-ASHFIELD   LILYWHITE LTD..
TRIANGLE, HALIFAX.

3. The church of St. Michael on Outram Street was built in two stages. The first phase, following plans by architect James Fowler, was begun in November 1886. The nave was added in 1909, allowing seating for 650 at a total cost of £7,000. Lilywhite of Halifax published this card in the early 1920s.

INTRODUCTION

The purpose of this book is to portray Sutton-in-Ashfield and Huthwaite through the medium of picture postcards, which were at the height of their popularity in Edwardian times – both as items on which to send messages and as pictures to collect.

Picture postcards were first published in Britain in 1894, but the idea did not really capture the public's imagination until 1902 when the Post Office altered their regulations so that the message could be written on the reverse and the whole of the front could be devoted to the picture. The next twelve years – up to the outbreak of the First World War – is termed the 'Golden Age' of Postcards when up to three million cards a day were sent. It is mainly from this period and the following 20 years that the illustrations for this publication were chosen.

Cards of Sutton-in-Ashfield and district were published by a mixture of local, county and national firms. Valentine of Dundee and W.H. Smith issued cards all over the country, only using scenes of towns with large enough populations to give their products a reasonable sale. From Nottingham, C. & A.G. Lewis provided excellent coverage of Sutton in the 1920s, and cards in the 'Peveril' (pre-1914) and 'Rex' (1920s) series also appeared. Local publishers to feature in this book include F.W. Buck of Sutton, H.G. Owston of Annesley, and the Sherwood Photographic Co. of Mansfield.

In the hurly-burly of late 20th century life, it is pleasant occasionally to stand back and wallow in a little nostalgia from a slower, earlier age.

David Ottewell
July 1993

Acknowledgements: thanks to Sutton Library for the loan of cards 6, 11-12, 18, 20-21, 24, 33-35 and 42.

Front cover: Low Street on a W.H. Smith-published card, posted to Kings Lynn in August 1914. The sender was working at Briggs & Co.'s shop in the Market Place *(see illus. 8)* "Arrived quite safe, have nice digs and think I shall be quite at home both at shop and digs. Working tonight, Sid." The "Denman's Head" Hotel is on the right, facing the old police station and the Nottingham and Notts bank. Market Street goes off to the left. People are able to congregate freely in the middle of the road without fear of being run over.

Back Cover (top): the tram terminus at Huthwaite. An open-topped tram waiting to load up and begin its return journey to Mansfield. The inclement British weather meant that many of these tramcar types were soon adapted to include a covered top deck. Card published by the Sherwood Photographic Co., and postally used in April 1911.

(bottom): Published by F.W. Buck & Sons, booksellers and stationers of Low Street, this card shows the old police station, built in Albert Square in 1861. Shortly after this card was posted in 1906, operations were transferred to the new building on Brookside. *(see illus. 17).*

The Cemetery and War Memorial, Sutton-in-Ashfield. No. 2744.

4. Opened on 24th May 1892, the cemetery was later chosen as the site of the town's war memorial. The chapel to the rear fell into disuse and was eventually demolished. C. & A.G. Lewis card from the 1920s, when William Hall was cemetery superintendent.

Sutton in Ashfield, No. 3845

5. The long-established local firm of Miller & Co. had their premises in the Market Place. They dealt in drapery and clothing. When this card was published by C. & A.G. Lewis in the early 1920s Miller & Co. were advertising their annual sale, "The Event of the Season", featuring an eye-catching arrangement of goods.

6. View of the Market Place taken before 1905 as the properties to the left of this picture were removed around that year in the reorganisation of the area. The shop with the advertising signs belonged to Childs the confectioners, while beyond it was the ironmonger's shop belonging to the Needham family.

7. This gathering in the Market Place outside the 18th century "Denman's Head" was captured by local photographer Ashley, though there is no indication on the card of when the occasion was or what its purpose was. Military uniforms are in evidence, and the card was sent to Bristol in July 1920.

8. The building on the right in this picture of the Market Place is the Town Hall, designed by J.P. Adlington and opened in 1889. It was built as a public hall rather than a place in which to conduct civic business. Fronting the Town Hall are the businesses of William Shaw, fancy draper and milliner, and Briggs & Co., boot and shoe makers

Low Street, Sutton-in-Ashfield.

9. Looking down Low Street from the Market Place in a similar view to illus. 5, but with fewer people in evidence. Local firm F.W. Buck & Sons published the card.

10. A later view of Low Street on a C. & A.G. Lewis card which was posted to Bradford in January 1921. On the right are Hiltons, boot and shoe dealers at no.2 Low Street, and Boots the chemists. A sign outside their shop advertises "national insurance dis-

pensing". On the lamp-post, a notice warns *"no vehicles allowed in the Market Square by order"*. The young boy by the van on the left is cleaning up horse manure (notice his hand-card in centre picture), a useful way of earning pocket money.

11. An early view of the "Unicorn" Inn on Low Street (to the rear of the small detached shop), whose proprietor at the time was George Hardy. It was later used by the Liberal Club, but has since been refurbished and the original inn name restored. The building on the left is the "Rifleman" Inn.

12. Low Street in 1928 on another C. & A.G. Lewis card, featuring the "Old Nag's Head" Inn before the present mock-Tudor building was put up on the same site to replace it *(see illus.14)*. W. Ward's tobacconists shop has a posse of signs advertising his wares.

13. The chemist's shop of Mr. Buckland was later taken over by Boots. Another Lewis postcard.

14. The mock-Tudor "Nag's Head" replaced the earlier building on the same site. Facing it is the "Rifleman", where, at the time Valentine published this card in the 1940s, Arthur Ansell was licensee. The tower in centre picture belonged to John Briggs; for many years this building was a chemist's shop.

PORTLAND SQUARE, SUTTON-IN-ASHFIELD.

15. A rather empty Portland Square with the tram-lines in the foreground and the extensive premises of outfitters William North at the far end of the square, which was named after the Dukes of Portland. W.H. Smith 'Kingsway' series postcard.

16. Looking down Brookside towards Low Street and the Market Place, showing on the left the premises of Martin Radford, optician, next to the substantial building of the old police station. The cottages facing it on the right have now all been demolished.

17. The police station on Brookside replaced their earlier premises on the corner of Low Street, and was much larger than its predecessor. In 1922 it was staffed by Harry Brooks (inspector), two sergeants and 16 constables; many of the signs outside are recruiting posters. The building ceased to be used as a police station in 1966.

18. 'Rex' series card of the public baths on Brookside, opened in 1924.

19. One of the main routes into Sutton, Outram Street took its name from the Outram family, who towards the end of the 19th century owned much of the land in the area. Before this, it had gone by the name of Tenter Lane.

20. The sender of this 'Rex' series postcard wrote *"I've marked the picture house"* (on the left), *known as the "Tivoli "*. She went on to say *"since this was taken, they've taken the tram standards and tramlines up"*. The tram service was discontinued in 1932.

Council Offices, Sutton in Ashfield. 1929, No. 3847

21. The Council Offices in 1929 on a C. & A.G. Lewis card. These were built in 1880 on Outram Street to the design of M.W. Bishop, council surveyor. The picture captures the council in patriotic mode, with a pair of union flags flanking the plaque. The site is now occupied by a bank.

22. A much later card (by Valentine), posted in Mansfield in June 1946, shows the Mansfield & Sutton Co-operative Society premises on the left. Opposite are the Jubilee buildings, in which the milliners' shop of Hilda Godfrey is prominent.

23. The Wesleyan Chapel on Outram Street was opened on 29th May 1883, and is seen here advertising "a grand bazaar". It was used as a place of worship for 85 years until closing in 1968.

24. Jarvis's Corner was on the corner of Outram Street and Forest Street, and named after a local family of stonemason's who ran their business from here. When C. & A.G. Lewis published this card, the site was for sale.

25. The name Priestsic Road derives from ancient times, when a priest's house was situated where this road and Top Green met. The house had a stream running nearby; the medieval word for this is 'sic'. The school in the middle distance was opened in 1900 at a cost of £9,410. C. & A.G. Lewis postcard.

26. A superbly-animated 1909 view c
scene at the junction with Penn Str
Mansfield, and is about to cross the C

eet on a Lewis postcard, showing a
no.15 is on its way into town from
n railway bridge.

27. A peaceful scene on Station Road, not much changed since this early 1920s photograph. The wall and railings to the left mark the boundary of the Croft School, and the houses beyond remain. To the right, the land has been taken over by garages and other industrial premises. Card by C. & A.G. Lewis.

28. C. & A.G. Lewis also published this card featuring a rural scene on Station Road with the solitary horse pulling its load of hay up from the direction of Sutton Junction and Coxmoor.

29. Dating from the beginning of the 19th century, Tower Mill was owned by William Downing Adlington. It stood overshadowing the railway station at Sutton Junction until it was destroyed by fire in 1917. Card in the 'Peveril' series.

30. Sutton Junction railway station on the Midland line between Mansfield and Nottingham was three-quarters of a mile from the town centre, where another station was sited, with a frequent service between these two and Mansfield. The station closed in October 1964, having been the first to open in the town 115 years previously.

31. The Midland's railway terminus in Sutton, one of four stations in the area (as well as the three illustrated, there was also a Great Central station). The Midland one here closed to passengers in September 1949.

32. The Great Northern's station, where passengers alighted for Huthwaite as well, was on the line from Nottingham to Shirebrook. In 1912, when this postcard was published, nine passenger trains in each direction called here daily, with two on Sundays. This station closed in September 1956.

33. Advertisements telling of such diverse delights as Campion Cycles, The Cunard Line, and the local Wakes week are stuck on the rear of Langford House, which looks out here onto Devonshire Square and the Bullring, last used for this purpose in 1832. C. & A.G. Lewis card no. 3840.

34. Dalesforth House. The writer of this card says *"Dear Annie, I expect you will know the old spot, can you pick any of them out?"* Of course, today, this area is all built up, and to stand in the middle of the road as these children were when they lined up for the photographer about 1908, would now be courting disaster!

35. A 'Rex' series postcard of the 1920s captures one man and his dog on a walk down a quiet Alfreton Road.

36. An unknown photographer took this view of King Street looking down towards the Market Place. Originally, this thoroughfare had been called Beggar Street, but the restoration of the monarchy in 1660 stimulated its present name. To the right are the premises of Charles Saxton, beer retailer, at no.41.

37. The Mansfield and District Light Railway began running trams in July 1905, and the service reached Sutton on 1st September that year. This view of a tram on Mansfield Road was taken by a C. & A.G. Lewis photographer near the junction of Lammas Road and Church Lane. The 4ft 8½ ins track ran almost down the centre of the road.

38. The Lawn Pleasure Grounds at Sutton-in-Ashfield provided a facility for local inhabitants. This Lewis card of the 1920s shows the bandstand.

39. The Unwin family, who were textile manufacturers at the Sutton Old Mill, built themselves a mansion on Forest Lane about 1760. This was demolished a century later, but the grounds, extending to nearly 20 acres, remained and were later turned into a park, with the mill dam as a centrepiece. Another Lewis postcard.

PARK AND MILL DAM. SUTTON-IN-ASHFIELD.

CROMPTON'S
PUBLISHERS

40. The old mill from which the stretch of water gets its name was situated on the far side of the water behind the trees that can be seen in the middle distance. Card published by Crompton's about 1915.

Parish Church Sutton-in-Ashfield.

Crompton's Publishers.

41. The parish church of St. Mary Magdalene has parts dating back to the twelfth century, but it was largely restored in 1868. The churchyard extends over four acres.

THE VICARAGE, SUTTON-IN-ASHFIELD.

42. J. Wilson, removal contractors, help to move a new incumbent into the vicarage. The reverse of the card carries testimonials for the firm from Rev. J.A. Adams (the vicarage, Mansfield), H.S. Shacklock (solicitor, market-place, Sutton), Rev. W.H.C. Stainer (curate, Sutton).

43. The corrugated iron building of St. Modwen's old church began life at St. Alban's, Sneinton, Nottingham, and was brought to Sutton and erected on Hardwick Street in 1886. It served there until a new St. Modwen's was opened on Station Road in 1937.

44. The origins of the congregational church at Sutton-in-Ashfield can be traced back to 1651, but the building seen on this anonymously-published card was only opened on 14th April 1906. It replaced a chapel which was demolished when the Market Place was extended at the beginning of this century. The architects were G. Baines & Son, London.

CHURCH OF "ST.JOSEPH THE WORKER",SUTTON-IN-ASHFIELD

45. The relatively modern church of St. Joseph the worker is shown on this card published by Valentine & Son of Dundee, and posted to Solihull in July 1965.

Ashfield Quartette Party.

Full Particulars, Apply
H. C. WRIGHT,
Kirkby Road, Sutton-in-Ashfield.

Brooklyn Press, Sutton.

46. In the 'Golden Age of Postcards' (1902-18), cards were often used for advertising
purposes. This one, issued by the Brooklyn Press, was for a local group of entertain-
ers.

HUTHWAITE

47. Sutton Road, Huthwaite, on a photographic card used in April 1926. The writer says *"we live at the back of the house with X. This view is looking towards Sutton-in-Ashfield"*. On the right is the Lyric Electric Theatre, where in 1922, Kendal Faraday Litchfield was proprietor.

TERMINUS, SUTTON ROAD, HUTHWAITE

48. Derby postcard publisher F. Scarratt produced this superb view of a Mansfield-Huthwaite tram at the western terminus of the line. The card was sent to Kettering in September 1911. *"I am going to a whist drive tonight"*, wrote Ida.

49. Historian E.L. Guilford was a little unkind to Huthwaite when he wrote at the turn of the century: *"there are few more depressingly sordid places in the county than this which stands close to the highest point (654 ft.) reached within our borders."* Main Street has not changed much from this 1909 view on a card published by H.G. Owston of Annesley Woodhouse.

50. Published by the Sherwood Photographic Co., Mansfield, this card shows what is now the "Workpeople's Inn" on the right. The building on the left has been demolished, and the "Peacock" Hotel stands on the site, but the house in middle distance, "The Beeches", remains today. Card sent to York in August 1910.

51. Common Road in 1913 on a postcard by H.G. Owston. The photographer has produced a nicely-balanced view, with plenty of children in the picture.

All Saints' Church, Hucknall Huthwaite. —BUCK AND SONS, PUBLISHERS.

52. The Duchess of Portland laid the foundation stone for All Saints Church on 22nd November 1902. It was built with rock brought up from a local colliery and has a dressing in Mansfield stone. Postcard by Buck and Sons of Sutton, dating from about 1910.

53. Known today as All Saints Church of England Infants, Common Road School was opened in 1891 with accommodation for 272 children, a selection of whom – carefully segregated by sex – appear to have mustered for the photographer on this card which was posted from Nottingham in November 1911.

54. The Council Schools on New Street were opened in 1902 with room for 360 boys and girls and 260 infants. Postcard by H.G. Owston of Annesley.

55. A prominent landmark on the road to Huthwaite from Sutton, the Wesleyan chapel, built in 1889, was the place where the Mansfield tram terminated. At the moment, the building is sadly neglected and up for sale. Photographic card from c.1910.

56. A view of the local cemetery seems a morbid postcard to send to anyone, but H.G. Owston provided one here. The cemetery and mortuary chapel was opened in 1889 and enlarged in 1912 when the keeper was William Pickaver Hardy.

57. Another card by Owston of Annesley, showing the primitive methodist chapel. At one time Huthwaite had one church and three chapels.

58. Hosiery manufacture was, along with mining, the principal work in the area in Edwardian times. This Owston card of c.1910 shows the new C.W.S. factory. Notice the unmade state of the road.

All Saints Church, Stanton Hill.

59. Stanton Hill is served by All Saints Church, built in 1899 using local stone. It cost £2,000 and had seating for 480 worshippers. The card was written by someone at Skegby vicarage and posted at Sutton in July 1915.